SHOW UP FILLED UP

HOW TO GET WHAT YOU WANT
OUT OF PEOPLE AND LIFE

KARY OBERBRUNNER

Illustrations by Leigha Sherman
Developmental Edit: Tina Morlock
Project Manager: Natalie Hanson
Cover Design: Debbie O'Byrne

ethos
collective

Printed in the United States of America

Illustrations by Leigha Sherman

Published by Ethos Collective™
PO Box 43, Powell, OH 43065
www.EthosCollective.vip

LCCN: 2021908786
Paperback ISBN: 978-1-63680-037-0
e-book ISBN: 978-1-63680-038-7

Available in paperback, hardcover, e-book, and audiobook

Dedication

For Skip Prichard and Dan Miller.
Thank you for Showing Up Filled Up in my life.

Contents

INTRODUCTION

Most People Show Up Empty

You become the ultimate outlier
by showing up filled up.

WARNING: This book reveals a powerful secret. This secret has allowed me to create the life of my dreams. It's made me millions of dollars, allowed me to ignite millions of souls, and connected me with celebrities and leading entrepreneurs in my industry. It has enabled me to be, do, and have more—and help more people—than I once imagined possible.

Those with noble motives leverage this secret in order to create wisdom and wealth. They use its incredible power to benefit humanity and make an impact on future generations. Those with selfish motives leverage this secret to manipulate people and secure money, sex, or power.

Understanding this secret's potential for abuse, some people dismiss it altogether, claiming it is simply too powerful—too dangerous—to apply or to share.

But that's a mistake.

Just like the gift of fire, this secret is a tool. We use it to light the world or burn down a forest. The outcome is completely up to you.

So what is the secret?

It's the hidden reason why people think what they think and do what they do. And if you understand this secret and use it for good, you can change your life.

You might even change your world.

Dig the well before you need it.

You may be familiar with the Chinese proverb that says, "Dig the well before you are thirsty." In our context for *Show Up Filled Up*, digging the well is building up influence, and it's something you must do *before* you need to leverage it.

This requires establishing trust and demonstrating value. You can't have influence without first developing a relationship or connection. And all of that takes time, which means you have to think ahead. You have to dig the well before you need it.

Here's an example of that principle in action. As a publisher, I've worked with thousands of authors, helping them successfully write, publish, and market their books. Endorsements are often an important component of a successful book. These blurbs allow authors to borrow someone else's credibility to lift their own, and they can be effective tools when it comes to promotion. Most books have them, and nearly *all* books need them.

But I've noticed that most authors don't think about obtaining endorsements for their books until right before it is time to go to print. They don't think ahead about building relationships and goodwill. And as a result, they end up asking for the gift of someone's time and credibility at the last minute. Requests get denied because of a lack of connection or simply lack of time.

Some authors do think ahead but approach the opportunity from a selfish mindset:

➔ Who can serve *my* purpose?
➔ Who can give *me* what I want?
➔ Who will help *me* reach my goals?
➔ Who will ensure *my* success?

When you publish a book—or launch a product, course, or business—it's natural to look around and imagine who can serve you in reaching your goals. But anyone who lives by a serve-me philosophy will come up short on relationships and short on riches. This is why the outcome for these authors is often the same: Their requests get denied (or worse, ignored) because they are asking the wrong questions with the wrong motives. They may have thought ahead about whom to ask for endorsements, but they failed to consider what it takes to build connection, value, and influence with those people.

Digging the well before you need it is as much about timing as it is about motives.

Zig Ziglar taught us, "If you help enough other people get what they want, you will get what you want." This perspective shifts the focus from ourselves to others, allowing us to build positive relationships, and often leads to greater connection, impact, and influence.

Dig the well *before* you need it. **I had to learn this the hard way**.

When I first started writing books several decades ago, I worked with a traditional publisher. It was a big enough task writing the book, so I hadn't even considered who might endorse it once I'd finished writing it.

My acquisitions editor exposed my ignorance one day when she asked me, "Who would you like to endorse your book?" Naturally, I named the biggest, most powerful influencers I could recall. She replied, "Everybody wants those people to endorse them. Do you actually know any of them? More importantly, do any of them know you?"

I went silent.

That day, I realized the powerful truth: I hadn't invested in other people. And because I showed up empty in many relationships, I had nothing to offer and nothing to draw upon.

That book came into the world—without endorsements from any influencers. (Thankfully, a few generous friends lent me their names for my back cover copy.) The experience taught me a lesson I've never forgotten. I promised myself I would never be in a position of relational deficit again. Since that time, I've made it my mission to *show up filled up* in every conversation, every exchange, and every relationship.

This choice changed my life and my luck—if you believe in such a thing. Personally, I believe I make my own luck, and my guess is that soon you will too.

Let your reputation precede you.

Showing up at the eleventh hour and asking a stranger to endorse your book (or to do anything for that matter) reeks of rudeness and sends the message that you're a taker, not a giver. Even if that's not true and you actually have noble motives, the poor planning labels you as a rookie.

Relationships shouldn't start with a request, nor should they end when a request is fulfilled. Think about your relationships and interactions with others: Are you more likely to honor a request made by someone who has created value for you or by a complete stranger? How excited are you to hear from someone who only calls when she needs something?

The truth is, we all prioritize social commitments based upon how much value the activity or the relationship holds for us. We make time for people and things we value. It's the reason we answer some calls on the first ring and let others go to voicemail. That doesn't mean some people are *better* than others. It simply means they have learned how to add value to their relationships.

So how do you create value?

Be a connector, not a climber.

When I was a teenager, I went to a party where the person I wanted to speak to was on the far side of a very crowded room. As I made my way across the room, I pushed past some people and ignored others. If it had been necessary, I would have climbed over people. I wanted to bypass everyone who stood in my way. No one else really mattered to me.

Immaturity and selfish motives are a wicked combination. It's a combo that shows up in other scenarios. You've probably experienced what it's like to feel *used*. It's the feeling of having someone act interested just to get what he or she wants. We learn early on how to recognize when someone isn't genuinely interested in us. We all intuitively know the difference between climbers and connectors.

This reminds me of an experience my friend had at an airport recently. He made a connection with the airline employee, and she responded with reciprocity.

My friend—and several other passengers—missed their connecting flight. It wasn't their fault, but a result of their initial flight arriving too late. Many of the other passengers let the airline employee know their frustration by yelling at her. They left the kiosk in disgust, forced to spend the night in a hotel because of the late hour and no more departing flights.

My friend felt horrible for the employee. He approached her and the desk with genuine empathy.

She looked up and said, "How can I help you?"

"Wow. Tough day. I'm sorry those passengers treated you that way," he said.

"Oh, it's fine," she replied. "I'm used to it."

"No, it's not fine," he said. "It's not your fault."

She made eye contact and let the compliment sink in. "Yeah, I guess you're right." She smiled. "Thanks for noticing. We tend to be the bearers of bad news, and people have a knack for reminding us they don't appreciate it."

"I can't imagine," he said.

"Well, that's in the past now. How can I help you?"

"I don't expect it's even possible," he said, "but I have an early morning meeting with a very important client. Is there any way I could make it in time?"

My friend waited patiently while the airline agent typed away on her keyboard for about a minute and then looked up.

"It seems as though I found a solution. We can't have you miss that important meeting. I've rebooked you for another flight with a different airline that boards in ten minutes. I've upgraded you to first class."

My friend thanked her and asked if he could submit a customer review for her excellent service. She said it was unnecessary, but after a little more coaxing, she gave him the link to post his thoughts.

As soon as he boarded his next flight, while still waiting in his seat before takeoff, he provided a detailed account of the fantastic service he received from the employee.

He was a connector, and he made a point to reciprocate value.

It's the little differences that make all the difference.

People often tell me how lucky they think I am because things always seem to go my way. I appreciate their insight, but I don't believe luck has anything to do with my success. I believe my success is the result of knowing the secret and applying the secret.

This secret of showing up filled up is about value and connection and influence, but it doesn't mean you need to perform grand gestures or massive acts of kindness. In life, it is often the little difference that makes all the difference.

Each day, you and I interact with dozens of people, whether that's online or in person. The next time you do, take a moment to observe how others act. You may notice several outcomes. Some people:

➔ Get hateful comments.
➔ Get helpful comments.
➔ Stir up drama wherever they go.
➔ Get favors wherever they go.

Chalk it up to luck, chance, good looks, or wealth, but there's something much different at play here. Why did that airline customer service agent find a quick solution for my friend?

It wasn't because he flirted with her, offered her money, or gave empty compliments. She helped him because he validated her. He invested a minute in appreciating her.

Think about the word *appreciate*. In the context of real estate, when a property appreciates, it increases in value. The same is true for people. When we show up filled up and express appreciation for other people, we literally increase the other person's self-worth. By raising their value, our value rises in their eyes. The normal, natural response when someone gives to us is to give back in truth.

Many studies demonstrate the power of reciprocity, including research done by Robert Cialdini, known as the leading social scientist in the field of influence. He believes "people will help you if they owe you for something you did in the past to advance their goals."[1] That is how reciprocity typically works. This is one reason why restaurant servers often bring a mint or fortune cookie at the same time they bring your food bill. Providing you with a small yet unexpected favor yields higher gratuity tips.

Little differences make all the difference.

Make people feel special, and they will remember you.

Learning to show up filled up changes your life and the lives of those you meet. In a way, it's similar to a farmer sowing seeds. You might forget where you've invested "value seeds," but the people who receive them never do.

I've run into men and women who tell me how a word of encouragement I gave them at a critical time in their life decades ago has stuck with them. In their own words, it changed the trajectory of their lives. Although I've forgotten what I said, they never did. These "value seeds" yielded an incredible harvest.

I shouldn't be surprised. This pattern has been true for me too. Key people invested in me when I was short on self-belief. A man named Carl Muenzmaier changed my life when he wrote me a letter back in 1995 when I was just eighteen. Although I hadn't ever met him, his letter told me that God was going to use my life, and I should not give up. I was fresh off three tough trials, and I felt like checking out of life, possibly even through suicide. His simple letter made all the difference and renewed my will to keep living.

Decades later, in 2014, I was a few weeks out from launching my book *Day Job to Dream Job*. A "friend" living in another country lied about me to advance his own career. His behavior was a strategic, calculated attempt to get me out of the way so he could get ahead.

His betrayal crushed me.

The next day, a different friend introduced me to John Lee Dumas via email. I knew there was something special about this stranger when he emailed me back. Although I had nothing to give him in return, he shared his growing platform with me and promoted *Day Job to Dream Job* via his podcast, *Entrepreneurs on Fire*. I never forgot his kindness, and when he released his book in 2021, *The Common Path to Uncommon Success*, I made it a point to reciprocate value by helping him launch it.

Showing up filled up can be used for good or evil. You must decide what kind of life you want to live: a noble one that honors everyone with whom you come in contact or a selfish one that takes advantage of others.

Start today by deliberately making people feel special wherever you go, both the loved ones in your life and the strangers you meet along the way. Even the thirty-second interaction with the cashier at your local grocery store can shift his destiny.

Add value to others whenever you go. When you do, these people will do the same for you.

Are you ready to show up filled up? If so, let's begin.

CHAPTER 1

Everybody Wants Something

You understand all people have unique needs, dreams, and goals.

When attending meetings with my colleagues early on in my career, my focus was on myself—how I wanted the meeting to go and what I wanted out of it. Then one day, I made a conscious switch: When others were speaking, I closed my mouth and *listened* to what they were saying. I didn't shut up to think. I shut up to listen and observe. I stopped thinking about my next move and what I wanted to say, and I focused on the person speaking. I listened to my team members' words and paid attention to their body language.

What I discovered that day changed my life and my business. I was blown away by how much understanding happens simply by getting quiet, focusing on the other person, and really listening.

In most conversations, people aren't listening to learn—they're listening to respond. Or they aren't listening at all because they're so busy thinking about their rebuttal. I have certainly been guilty of that in the past.

What about you?

The practice of listening and observing gives all parties a payoff at the end of the day. Placing a priority on the other person's needs expresses genuine care and concern. When people can see that you sincerely care about them and what they have to say about their hopes, dreams, and goals, they will often reciprocate.

How do you make the shift to being focused on others?

First, finely tune your observation skills. What do people *really* want? What are their needs and expectations? Watch for the signs that show you what people hope for and dream about. I promise you—those signs are there.

Observation is an active practice. It requires your eyes and ears as well as your heart. Part of growing and maturing is learning how to actively listen to and observe the people around you. Learn to do it well, and your communication will improve tremendously. Master this discipline, and the people around you will feel heard, seen, and cared for, and they will respond differently to you as a result.

Everybody wants something. Developing the ability to recognize people's desires—and then putting their desires and needs before your own—is essential to showing up filled up.

Do you pick up the signs?

We all have unique superpowers. One of mine is noticing small details. When my team and I meet on Zoom for video conferencing, I notice haircuts, the book titles on the shelves behind them, and other details that others might miss at first glance. This odd talent is one I've deliberately honed, and it has proved to be extremely valuable. Here's what I mean.

Several years ago, a client asked me to evaluate his website during one of our coaching sessions.

As I clicked through the pages on his site, I asked him to tell me who his ideal client was.

"Business executives," he replied.

Stopping at his photo, I said, "This won't do."

"What? Is it my shirt? Or my hair?" he asked anxiously. "My glasses?"

"Nope," I responded.

"Then what is it?" he asked.

"I don't believe you."

I went on to explain. I told my client the photo reminded me of a conversation between Sam Phillips and Johnny Cash in the movie *Walk the Line*. At his audition, Johnny sang someone else's song. During the sad attempt at a gospel tune, Sam interrupted him and declared that the audition was over. Johnny pushed back, asking why.

"I don't believe you," Sam replied in an icy tone.

Johnny had sung the words correctly. He had played the music perfectly. And still, it was all wrong because it lacked believability. The song wasn't true for *him*, so the performance didn't connect.[1]

I asked my client again, "Who's your target market?"

Again, he told me business executives.

"Look at your watch. How much did it cost?"

I already knew the answer. Not much.

Personally, I couldn't care less about the price of his watch. But business executives would. He wanted a high-end, high-dollar client, but his photograph didn't match up with what those potential clients would demand from him. They wouldn't believe him because his words didn't match his image.

Because I slowed down long enough to pay attention to the details, I observed his disconnect. Because I listened to his goals, I knew the kind of confidence he needed to attract executives. My client changed the photograph on his website immediately. Shortly after, he had a waiting list for potential clients interested in his executive coaching services.

"You see, but you do not observe."

In "A Scandal in Bohemia" by Sir Arthur Conan Doyle, a scene between Sherlock Holmes and Watson illustrates the reality most people fail to observe.

> "When I hear you give your reasons," I [Watson] remarked, "the thing always appears to me to be so

ridiculously simple that I could easily do it myself, though at each successive instance of your reasoning, I am baffled until you explain your process. And yet I believe that my eyes are as good as yours."

"Quite so," he answered, lighting a cigarette, and throwing himself down into an armchair. "You see, but you do not observe. The distinction is clear."[2]

Holmes went on to point out the distinction. Watson had walked up and down a particular set of stairs hundreds of times, but he did not know precisely how many steps it took to get from the bottom to the top. "You have not observed. And yet you have seen. That is just my point. Now, I know that there are seventeen steps because I have both seen and observed."

Watson, like most people, had failed to develop his observation skills. On the other hand, Sherlock Holmes had refined this skill into a superpower of noticing every little detail. That trait, in fact, was what made him such a brilliant detective.

You don't have to be a private detective to strengthen your observation skills. When it comes to applying this skill to your relationships, it is a matter of paying attention to the details. Listen intently when people talk. Pay attention to what lights them up and to what brings them down. Fine-tune your ability to observe, and you will soon be able to discover others' unique needs—even if they don't explicitly tell you.

Does the video match the audio?

The powers of observation come in handy in my business in other ways. Recently, for example, one of my clients saw that another influencer in his space had quickly gained two million followers. When I investigated the *influencer's* profile, I wasn't as impressed as my client.

"He bought those followers," I said. "They're fake."

The influencer appeared to have an impressive number of followers, but the lack of engagement on his content told a different story. The video (what my client saw) didn't match the audio (what the engagement was saying, which wasn't much). Only two people had commented on his recent posts. If he really had two million authentic, engaged followers, he would have had more comments and interaction.

My observation helped my client focus on his work and stop worrying about being behind in the social media game. Rather than getting caught up with the need to compete (with what turned out to be fabricated success), he focused his attention on the opportunities he had right in front of him to engage with his followers and make an impact on their lives with his message.

The lesson here is twofold: 1) Take time to observe beyond the obvious. Make sure the audio matches the video. 2) Keep your focus on the people who matter most to you and your business. That focus will empower you to show up filled up and make a more significant difference in people's lives.

Beneath the mask, there's a deep need.

When I took a little more time to examine the influencer who had caught my client's attention, I noticed two desires:

1. He wanted more influence and impact.

2. He wanted to grow his influence and impact quickly.

The trouble was, he didn't know how to increase his influence (desire 1) as fast as he wanted (desire 2). So he took a shortcut and purchased followers to make himself look more successful than he was. When I revealed the truth to my client, he became less trusting of someone he had begun to admire. Inauthenticity will do that.

This influencer was not showing up filled up. His carefully crafted social media façade *continues* to keep him from growing his impact. And he isn't alone. When trying to grow our platforms, most of us can relate to the frustration that builds when we can't quickly achieve our goals. We follow suit by putting on masks that *project* self-sufficiency and *protect* our self-image. But here's the truth: Hiding behind a mask of perfection repels people, and it makes you unrelatable.

Showing up filled up means removing our masks, an action few people are brave enough to do. But the battle of our ego is won in surrender.

Authenticity is the only way forward. Removing your mask requires vulnerability. True vulnerability is so rare that when people encounter it, it attracts them like a moth to a flame.

Only someone showing up filled up can admit they're empty and need some time to refuel. It's a paradox. In your weakness, you are strong.

Listen with your eyes.

Our eyes process an incredible amount of data every second they are open. The key to listening with your eyes is *focus*. When we embody laser-like focus, everything else around us grows dim. This kind of focus requires getting quiet and letting go of our own agenda long enough to truly listen.

I attended a conference in London a few years ago featuring many industry-leading international speakers on a gorgeous stage. After speakers' sessions, many of the attendees rushed to meet them, get their books signed, and praise them on their presentation. Nothing's wrong with that approach, but I chose a different strategy.

Standing back from the pressing crowd, I waited patiently. I knew each speaker had a need, and my help would go much further than an impulsive compliment.

Approaching the first speaker, I said, "I truly enjoyed your message. It clearly impacts people. I see you've published a book. Are you happy with the results you're getting in the international market?"

Then I shut up and listened to what they had to say. I didn't need to sell myself or my services. I didn't need to make the conversation about me. Rather, I showed up filled up, ready to meet their needs.

The first speaker said, "No. I'm not happy with the results. Can you help?" Over the next three days, I repeated this process with nearly every one of the speakers. They each gave me their business card and asked me to follow up with them after the conference, with the hope I would represent them and their books in the foreign market.

Years before, the outcome would have unraveled quite differently. I would have gone up to these speakers, introduced *myself*, and told them *my* profession, *my* credentials, and *my* results.

Notice the pattern? *Me. Me. Me.*

Big mistake!

I would have shown up empty and left empty-handed. In ignorance, I would have positioned myself as forgettable and then a year later wonder why none of those speakers did business with me. I chose, instead, to listen, focusing on each of them intently as they spoke to me about their books' successes or failures and the struggles they were dealing with in marketing their message.

All day long, people approached those speakers with their own agendas in mind. I chose to *listen* rather than talk. I made them my center of attention in the moments we shared during that conference, and I followed up and responded to their needs after the conference. Today, I'm happy to call them friends—and even happier to have them as satisfied clients.

CHAPTER 2

People Can't Articulate What They Want

*You invest time and energy to
build sincere rapport.*

In Chapter 1, we learned everyone wants something. But ready for the irony? Most people can't tell you what they want. Here's a major reason why. In my book *Unhackable*, I share some alarming data:

- Human knowledge doubles every twelve hours.

- We encounter 5,000 ads a day.

- We make 35,000 decisions a day.[1]

No wonder we struggle with clarity. Distractions abound, and notifications interrupt our best intentions. We live in a world that surrounds us with chaos and confusion.

Clarity attracts. Confusion repels.

Many years ago, I joined an international coaching program. Like me, most of my colleagues were beginners in their careers. Professional coaching and speaking for a fee were activities we didn't do much, so we tried to soak up as much of our mentors' knowledge as we could.

Whenever we gathered on the coaching calls with our mentors, most people fought to get their "questions" answered. The truth is, my colleagues often didn't know what their question was. They talked in circles trying to uncover their needs and formulate their thoughts into questions. The process wasted a ton of time, and it was agonizing for the colleague, the mentors, and everyone else who listened to the group coaching call.

There's little I hate more than wasting time—mine or anyone else's. So after hearing a few people rabbit-trail their way to a semi-coherent question, I determined to use my time with the mentors as wisely and efficiently as possible. I committed to identifying my question before I jumped on the group coaching calls. Because it wasn't something I was used to, I had to get quiet days before the call, and disconnecting from the noise and busyness of life required discipline.

Still, I knew showing up filled up meant valuing my mentors' time, my colleagues' time, and my time.

My goal was to clarify my question in its simplest form before I got on the weekly call. During the days between the coaching calls, I invested time in peeling back the layers of my mental and emotional ambiguity. I wanted to maximize not only my time with my mentor but also the overall impact of the coaching session for myself and anyone else on the call. I realized that the clearer I could be in my question, the more time we had to hash out challenges and chip away at barriers to my success.

My hard work paid off.

The mentors who took my coaching questions often commented about the depth of my request. They appreciated the clarity and the effort that went into identifying my question.

But my learning and move toward intentional clarity didn't stop when the call ended.

I wrote down their replies and then referred back to my notes as I applied their advice to my actions throughout the week. On the following week's coaching call, I showed up filled up. I regularly reported how the mentor's advice on the previous call enabled me to get closer to success. I shared my progress, my obstacles, and my new awareness.

While I didn't set out to become an influencer in this circle of coaches, this quickly became my reality. The colleagues who heard me on the group coaching calls soon came to me with their questions. They witnessed my clarity firsthand and the breakthroughs in my business week after week.

Their curiosity pushed them to inquire about my books and my programs. Many of them signed up for my products and services. I guess they figured, "If Kary can do it, then I can do it too." Several mentors even pursued me off-line and hired me for my writing, publishing, and marketing services. In their own words, they appreciated my strategic thinking and bias for action. They wanted someone like me working on their branding and business.

Casual observers commented that I was lucky, saying things like, "You're always at the right place at the right time." Few know the real secret—that even on coaching calls, where I was technically the client, I committed to showing up filled up and adding value to my mentors, my colleagues, and myself.

Let people think what they want. Focus on getting clear about your goals, your message, and what you need to do to show up filled up. And then watch how your clarity cuts through the confusion and attracts people to you.

Leverage the need to feel heard.

Be prepared for a variety of responses when people see your success. You might even encounter a "hater" who speaks with deep-seated envy, anger, or malice if for no other reason than they want to be heard.

Have you ever received an email from a hater?

I have, and I can tell you from experience that even if you don't know the person, their hurtful comments can threaten your courage and leave you feeling empty. No one likes criticism, and we're especially vulnerable to it when starting something new—whether it's a book, service, or product. In those early days, we often give negative words too much weight. We may even let them hold us back.

When I was just starting to see some success in my business, I received several emails from haters, and I didn't know how to respond. My friends and mentors told me to ignore the negative emails and their senders, but I felt like these people deserved to be acknowledged.

Although I didn't need to defend my actions, I wanted these people to know their feelings were important and that their thoughts mattered to me. I responded calmly, acknowledging their point of frustration or anger, even if I disagreed with them. Some of the people ignored my response. But a few of these so-called "haters" responded with a sincere "thank you."

As I engaged with the haters who responded to my acknowledgment of them and their claim, I noticed they shared something in common. Each ultimately admitted that they were struggling with something else: a divorce, financial pressures, or the death of a loved one. Their initial comment to me contained anger, but the anger was not directed at me. Not really. I was simply on the receiving end of it, an outlet for their angst, a release valve for their pressure.

When I replied and acknowledged them and their pain, many of these same people responded with genuine gratitude. I gave them exactly what they truly wanted: assurance that they were not alone.

It is only possible to respond to a hater with kindness when we show up filled up. If we are hanging on to any feeling of entitlement or insecurity or are simply exhausted or overwhelmed, we're likely to lash out at the hater with a self-justified response of, "Who do you think you are? How dare you!"

As you might expect, I haven't gotten this right every time—and still don't. There have been plenty of times I've shown up empty and responded from a place of lack, scarcity, and fear. Regrettably, that kind of response has had the same effect as tossing gasoline on smoldering coals.

Relational explosions!

Such was often the case when I first started in the business world. Back then, my self-worth was low at best. Rather than simply listen to people's grievances, I slipped into defensive mode. Because I didn't have any self-confidence to spare, every interaction became a battleground. If I lost an argument, it was a death blow to my ego. Therefore, I fought to preserve and protect the fragile sense of self-worth I had tied to my business.

Slinging cruel or even passive-aggressive words back at a hater will accomplish nothing. In doing so, we abdicate our power and allow other people's opinions to shape our self-image.

Whenever you enter a relationship needy, you always walk out empty. No person can fill the hole inside your heart. But when you do the deep work to show up filled up, the opposite is true.

When I'm intentional about showing up filled up, then I don't need outside validation or approval. By reminding myself that I am whole and full, I allow the overflow of my heart to spill abundance into others. When I show grace and kindness, these haters will many times reciprocate grace and kindness. Over the years, a time or two, they've even turned into right-fit clients and our most loyal advocates.

Like clarity, your strong sense of self-worth and confidence will radiate believability and attract even greater levels of success.

Ask for permission to ask questions.

One reason it's so tempting to pop off at haters is that no one enjoys unsolicited advice. Even if the hater's comment is valid, its source and timing make us discount its value.

In fact, even when we receive unsolicited advice as constructive criticism from someone who sincerely cares about us, it can be difficult to accept graciously.

Knowing that I don't relish people telling me what I *should* do, I practice an important habit with my clients. Before I take on the role of a truth-teller, I first ask them permission to ask questions.

When you start your communication with the intention of understanding the other person and her goals, you set the conversation up for success. Right out of the gate, you show respect for the other person.

In contrast, if you dive right into what's wrong and how you think the other person should fix it, the person may misinterpret your unsolicited advice. You may come across as trying to fix the *person* rather than the *problem*. And if the person feels threatened by your unsolicited comments, he or she is likely to dismiss it as bad advice.

By showing up filled, you flip the equation. Asking for permission, instead of giving unwanted advice, gives the person the responsibility and the power to receive and respond to whatever comes next.

No one has ever refused my request for permission to ask a question. Humans are too curious! We possess an innate desire for clarity.

Think about it. What if someone asked you, *May I have your permission to ask you a question?*

Are you going to say no?

Not likely. You want to know what the question is.

That's human nature. And the people you approach with this questioning are going to react the same way, which will open the door for you to offer insight based on their thoughtful responses.

What about the rare person who says "no" and denies you the right to ask questions? They may be the type of person who prefers ignorance, or perhaps the timing is simply not right. In either case, move on. Respect their answer and don't waste their time or yours.

But with every person who responds with a yes to your request, you have an opportunity. You already know the person is open to growth. You simply need to ask the right question.

Very often, the next question I ask is both difficult and disarming: *What do you want?*

Let them sit with their confusion.

As I've mentioned, everybody wants *something*. Ironically, we don't always know exactly what we want. In fact, most of the time, we *don't* know. But until you know what the other person wants, you can't truly help them.

This is why after asking the disarming question (What do you want?), I get incredibly quiet. I don't rescue the other person by speaking. I let them sit with their confusion. This takes self-restraint and requires that I show up filled up.

When we show up empty, we're preoccupied with our own thoughts. We rush to fill in the silence. We care more about ourselves than the other person. But when we show up filled up, our self-confidence negates the need to speak.

As that silence builds, the other person realizes we don't need anything from them. Instead of using their words to fill the space, they must dive deep into themselves to find the answers.

Their confusion pushes them closer to that point of clarity, whether they realize it or not. In this moment, you've allowed them to cross from *unconscious incompetence* into *conscious incompetence*. Discovering what they want is now their puzzle to solve, and they won't relent until they put the pieces together.

They will realize their need.

Now, they can either walk away aware of their problem or confront the reality they need help.

In *The Matrix*, this was Neo's experience. His mentor, Morpheus, commented, "What you know you can't explain, but you feel it. You've felt it your entire life, that there's something wrong with the world. You don't know what it is, but it's there, like a splinter in your mind, driving you mad."[2]

Shifting from confusion to clarity about what they want creates a splinter, a discontent with the status quo. And with that splinter firmly planted in their minds, they can no longer rest until they've answered the question—not for you, but for themselves. This is the threshold of all transformation.

CHAPTER 3

Find Out What People Want

*You do the deeper work of getting
below the surface.*

The founder of Toyota, Kiichiro Toyoda, liked to ask questions. He modeled this within his company. Questions often function as the key that unlocks our ambiguity. He revolutionized the way we look at problem-solving, much in part to his father, Sakichi, an inventor. Sakichi is best known for his philosophy of asking questions.[1]

His process for solving a problem was quite simple: "Ask 'why' five times about every matter."

Below is an example of how asking *why* leads to a solution in the manufacturing process:

1. Why did the robot stop? *The circuit has overloaded, causing a fuse to blow.*

2. Why is the circuit overloaded? *There was insufficient lubrication on the bearings, so they locked up.*

3. Why was there insufficient lubrication on the bearings? *The oil pump on the robot is not circulating sufficient oil.*

4. Why is the pump not circulating sufficient oil? *The pump intake is clogged with metal shavings.*

5. Why is the intake clogged with metal shavings? *Because there is no filter on the pump.*

The key to showing up filled up is to be infinitely curious about everything. By asking more questions, we can get much closer to helping others figure out what they truly want.

Get curious.

Over the past two decades, I've been blessed to have Chet Scott as my coach initially, then my colleague, and now my close friend. Chock-full of unorthodox techniques, Chet has an uncanny knack for getting to the heart of the matter. One of his main strategies is summed up in three short words: "Tell me more."

Chet believes there's always more to the story, and our tendency is to hold back on telling it. We all need an invitation to go deeper, hence the reply, "Tell me more." In his book *Becoming Built to Lead,* he says:

> It is my job to challenge [you] from belief, not frustration. I challenge [you] and every client early and often. I challenge because I believe. I challenge because I care. I challenge because I'm aiming at excellence and am comfortable telling hard, tough truth. I challenge because I've been challenged and seen the healthy, helpful effects.[2]

Chet challenges me to go below the surface. He is a master at creating those painful splinters that spur me toward change. But his motives are good. He's trying to reveal something I might not have realized on my own.

I've learned from Chet that loving people means not letting them off the hook. Growth requires a willingness to push for more, no matter how painful and challenging this process becomes, even if it takes saying, "Tell me more," five or ten times.

If we go deep enough, we will find the truth. Sincere questions act as a mirror, a subtle but strong reminder that the only way forward is through our discomfort. Staying with someone long enough to get to the heart of the issue also requires stamina, which means, of course, that you have to show up filled up, curious and ready to keep saying, "Tell me more."

Be confident, not arrogant.

Think back to a time when you felt like you had something to prove.

How did you feel about yourself, your work, or your product?

In all likelihood, you felt protective, perhaps overprotective, and sensitive to any perceived criticism. In those times, you probably craved *external validation*—for someone to boost your shaky sense of self-confidence and tell you that you were doing a good job and that you had value.

When we tie our worth to external confidence boosters, we do so from a place of scarcity. The prevalent and undermining feeling that drives our actions is that what we have or who we are isn't enough. We need to do more, have more, or be more, so we demand others' respect or approval to push us up the ladder of success.

This behavior comes with a cost. People feel the pull. They know when they're being used to increase our egos.

John Maxwell said, "True leadership cannot be awarded, appointed, or assigned. It comes only from influence, and that cannot be mandated. It must be earned. The only thing a title can buy is a little time—either to increase your level of influence with others or to undermine it."[3]

Bottom line: Authentic validation is a result of showing up filled up. It's a gift given freely by others when we create true value.

Have you ever met someone who demands an incredibly long introduction before he or she steps onto a stage to speak? Or have you come across people who insist on being addressed by fancy titles?

Both examples demonstrate a preoccupation with self rather than others. These people need the validation of titles because they don't *feel* worthy or confident in themselves. The result of their lack of confidence is arrogance. (Side note: I've heard it said that if you're a good speaker, you don't need an important title, and if you're a bad speaker, an important title won't help.)

Arrogance focuses on what others can do for you. Confidence focuses on what you can do for others. The arrogant person demands respect, while the confident person doesn't need others' approval or validation to continue doing what is right. He or she presses forward, takes action, and reaches out to help others along the way. In doing so, this person *earns* others' respect.

Arrogance results from showing up empty and expecting others to fill you up. Confidence results from showing up filled up and pouring into others.

It's not about you.

Notice the difference. Confident people focus on others, while arrogant people turn the focus back on themselves. Arrogant people expect everyone to serve them, while confident people have the ability to serve others.

Imagine visiting a doctor who shows up empty. You're experiencing back pain, so you schedule an appointment with a medical professional. You expect to be helped, so how would you feel if your doctor responded by saying, "How weird! My back has been hurting in the same exact place lately. Let me tell you all about it." You would probably label that doctor as someone with a bad bedside manner and never return.

We see the irony with the doctor's office example, but most of us miss the examples that pop up in our everyday lives. The truth is most people treat conversations like tennis matches.

You say something.

I say something back.

I say something else, and then you return with a reply. We volley comments back and forth and call it a conversation.

But when you show up filled up, the conversations go much differently. Chet Scott engages his clients in an activity called "7 Good Minutes."[4] This is how it goes:

1. Each person in the group pairs up with a partner.

2. One of the partners sets the clock for seven minutes.

3. For the duration of the timer, one partner keeps asking the other partner curious questions about their life. The conversation is completely one-sided.

4. When the clock stops, they switch roles.

When you try this activity, you'll be surprised by how much you learn about the other person, no matter how long you've known him or her. In fact, one time when I tried this activity, I learned more about the other person in seven minutes than I did the entire seven years of our relationship!

We touched earlier on the importance of active listening when it comes to showing up filled up. The 7 Good Minutes exercise is a tool you can use to develop your listening ability. When you use it regularly, you'll discover that your conversations will begin to reveal more about the other person, which will put you in a position to achieve brand-new depths in your relationships.

Be interested, not interesting.

When you aren't interested in what the other person has to say, seven minutes can seem like an eternity.

My advice? Be interested.

I offered similar advice to an audience member who asked an unexpected question during a question-and-answer time at a conference.

She asked, "How do I act like I'm interested in my clients?"

My reply was simple: "You don't *act*."

People can spot a fake, someone who's putting on a show just to get something in return. We all know if someone is truly interested. The way you listen and engage with them communicates everything they need to know. Showing up filled up means asking sincere questions and listening actively to what they have to say.

Everybody wants to be interesting. We all want people to *want* to listen to us. But when we focus on capturing others' attention or making ourselves the center of the conversation, we turn people off. We become wildly *uninteresting* and easy to ignore.

Think about it: You've heard people try to make themselves appear interesting by name-dropping, talking about their accomplishments, or spinning long, self-aggrandizing stories. You've been on the receiving end of these one-sided conversations, so you know they can be a *major* turnoff.

Don't make that mistake.

Focus on being *interested* instead of being *interesting*. When you do, people will want to talk to you. More than that, they may end up saying to you, "Tell me more." When that happens, you'll know they find *you* interesting.

Don't do dual relationships.

In the counseling profession, the term *dual relationships* is not a good thing.

The relationship between therapist and client is supposed to be one-sided. Although the counselor may appear to be the patient's friend, professional boundaries must be clearly set.

Counselors are held to a strict ethical protocol that prevents them from receiving gifts, attending events, or becoming otherwise personally involved with their clients. Crossing these lines can create a one-sided codependency between the counselor and the patient that creeps into dangerous territory if the counselor doesn't honor professional ethics.

In the business world, we don't have this strict code of ethics like therapists and other medical professionals. But there's still a danger of creating codependency that conflicts with our main goal of showing up filled up. I've seen this happen two different ways:

1. *The person you're helping becomes dependent upon your help.* Of course, the goal is to help people, but it needs to be executed in a way that allows them to learn how to be self-sufficient. You know the old adage, "If you give a man a fish, you feed him for a day. If you teach a man to fish, you feed him for a lifetime." For both parties to truly get what they want and need, you must teach others to fish. This way, they can also show up filled up for others and grow their influence, impact, and income.

2. *You become dependent upon others to help you in return.* By its very definition, this is not showing up filled up. In such settings, you have a motive for helping the other person. This is often revealed to others when there is an understated quid pro quo. Of course, the natural effect

of helping others get what they want is that you will also get what you want. This must happen organically. It cannot be forced.

Although it often yields a quick positive effect, learning how to show up filled up is a long-game strategy. For the secret to work smoothly, you must understand that dreams, goals, and wishes are not granted overnight through only one action. Rather, success is an accumulation of everything you do to help others.

Showing up filled up is a way of life.

When the world sees that you have a sincere desire to make others' dreams come true, things will start happening for you.

Some people will call it luck.

But you'll know the truth because you know the secret.

CHAPTER 4

Help People Get What They Want

You find great pleasure in solving people's problems.

Has someone ever told you that *you* are his or her hero?

It feels good, doesn't it? Even if the statement was made half-jokingly in response to a simple action, like holding the door or moving something heavy, it's nice to feel helpful.

When it comes down to it, we all need a little help now and then. We all *need* a hero.

My friend Dan Sullivan believes we can all *be* a hero to someone else.

Maybe you aren't feeling very heroic these days. If you think you have to make a grand gesture to be a hero, go back a few sentences. Carrying something heavy for someone may not be a big deal to you, but it might be to the person you're helping—especially if they know they can't carry the load on their own.

Seemingly small things can make a big difference, particularly if you are solving someone's problem. We've already explored how showing up filled up in life makes you more attuned to people's needs and problems. In this chapter, we'll move from awareness to action.

Before we dive in, I want to acknowledge the fact that the idea of solving other people's problems may overwhelm you. Everybody has problems, and there is only one of you. Don't despair. Being the hero doesn't necessarily mean you are the one doing the work. Here are just a few ways you can move to hero status:

- Your active listening skills can help people find a solution on their own.

- You can connect the person to a friend or colleague who is a better fit to help the person in need.

- You can teach people a skill or tip so they can solve the problem.

- You can provide a valuable resource that leads to a resolution.

- You can model how you solved a similar problem yourself.

Bottom line: Don't worry if you can't solve a problem directly.

Build rapport before you take the risk.

Nobody likes a "know-it-all." The person who has all the answers tells everyone what to do or constantly corrects others—all under the guise of helping.

The paradox is people who flex their intellectual muscles to gain attention or respect usually suffer from poor self-esteem. They may act like they know everything, but in reality, they feel insecure, which is why they have the need to steal the spotlight.

Only confident people can share the spotlight with others or include others in the decision-making, solution-finding process. These people don't feel the need to rush to be right.

Confident people, people who show up filled up, know before anyone is willing to take advice from them, they must first establish trust. And that starts with rapport.

A mentor of mine often says, "It's easier to kiss when someone is leaning in." His odd, but accurate observation conveys the fact that rapport closes the relational distance. Taking that observation a little further, I'm sure you've seen a movie or television show where one person goes in for a kiss, and the other person turns away quickly, allowing a peck on the cheek instead.

In the same way, offering solutions without first establishing rapport misses the mark. Taking that risk can leave you both feeling awkward, and it may even backfire and jeopardize the future of your relationship.

So how do you establish rapport? Sometimes it's as easy as putting your memory to work.

Remember relevant details.

Many people claim they have a poor memory. Such claims aren't completely accurate. Memory is similar to a muscle—and if you don't use it, you lose it. When you do use it, you strengthen it.

If you struggle remembering names and details, start writing them down. If you are like most people, you are rarely more than five feet away from your smartphone. That means you almost always have the ability to capture notes and reminders.

The next time you meet someone, create a voice memo or type a note immediately after the encounter. Capture any and all relevant information, from the person's name to a favorite food or book if they happen to mention it. If it seemed important to them in the conversation, it's worth remembering. The simple act of capturing the details will strengthen your memories about the person. Even if you never go back to the digital note, you are more likely to remember the details if you take the time to record it. And if you do forget, your phone will remember for you.

Consider medical professionals. During appointments, they record relevant details. When someone else comes to help the patient, they have all the pertinent information available to them. Recording the information could save a life—literally. Nobody wants their doctor to forget they're allergic to penicillin.

For our purposes, the relevant details we need to remember probably aren't life-threatening, but they could be life-transforming. Here's an example to illustrate what I mean:

My friend Shannon Waller has a unique hobby. Not long ago, I was in a Strategic Coach® break-out meeting with her and two other professionals whom I had never met before. Rather than focusing on myself or my agenda, I introduced the other two people to Shannon.

I said, "Shannon has a fascinating hobby that's somewhat uncommon. You probably wouldn't guess it, but she likes cutting down dead trees with a chainsaw." Then I asked Shannon to tell us more about it.

She explained that because her job is often cerebral, she enjoys working with her hands during her free time.

I wasn't revealing any secrets about my friend. She had actually posted about her hobby publicly on social media a few days prior. In sharing something interesting about her in the introduction, I put the attention on her and edified her in front of these new acquaintances. She's important to me, and she's brought incredible goodness to my life. I also demonstrated that I care enough to listen, pay attention, and value something unique about her. In that moment, she felt appreciated.

Appreciate.

Remember that word?

You should.

Think back to the introduction of this book. If you didn't read it (or don't remember it)—no judgment. But please read it now. Even if you did, please reread it again. Here's why: You've grown tremendously in these past few chapters. You're no longer the same person. You've gained new self-awareness, and you now have more to offer yourself, your friends, and the world around you. By rereading it, you'll understand it on a much deeper level.

Test me. You'll see.

Back to the word *appreciate*.

When a vehicle, plot of land, house, or piece of equipment appreciates, it grows in value. Some things appreciate naturally over time, but people—left to their own devices—tend to depreciate if they're not reminded of their worth. Just walking around in the world tends to chip away our self-worth.

When you remember relevant details about someone, you're endowed with an opportunity to increase his value with a sincere compliment. By appreciating someone, especially in the presence of others, you raise his value. The appreciated person believes several truths about you, including that you are trustworthy, benevolent, and valuable.

By showing up filled up with sincere verbal affirmation, you become more valuable in the eyes of the person receiving the compliment. This "relational glue" strengthens your bond and builds a bridge for you to enter the other person's world in a more significant way.

Build a database of givers.

Jotting down notes about our contacts and connections isn't a new idea. Ever hear of a Rolodex? (Some younger readers might need to do a Google search on the meaning of the word.)

Back in the day, people used these circular contraptions to keep track of their contacts. Thank goodness for technology—less space, less waste.

The right Rolodex held intrinsic value, something you guarded as a prized possession. This database recorded all the information you might need to know about an individual or business.

Hardly anyone uses physical Rolodexes anymore, but the concept is relevant to this conversation. We each have the power to build a database of givers. In the past decade, I've made it a point to do just this. Whenever I meet someone who embodies showing up filled up, I place them in my database. This person earns a spot as an influencer—someone I trust and someone I'm willing to trust with my friends and family.

I maintain this database because I can't—nor shouldn't—try to be a hero for everyone who needs help. I'm a genius in a few select areas, and I protect my genius zone by not diffusing my focus. This doesn't mean I can't offer help in other areas. Me helping means tapping into my database of givers.

Let's say one of my close friends has some key questions about investments or life insurance policies. This friend might say, "Kary, can you help me?"

I tell them, absolutely. Then I personally connect them with Kevin and Shana for investments or Will for insurance policies. Because I've earned a track record of showing up filled up for each of these people, I know when I connect them with my friend that they will take care of that friend, just like they take care of me.

It's a sacred trust—my database of givers. I do this with Daphne V. Smith, Niccie Kliegl, Tyler Wagner, and many others. My database of givers is one of my most valuable assets, much more important to me than any bank account or investment portfolio.

People who practice showing up filled up are gold. They bring incredible worth to the world by functioning in their genius zone.

One of the easiest ways I convey their worth is by protecting their time. Author and psychiatrist M. Scott Peck cautioned us, "Until you value yourself, you won't value your time. Until you value your time, you will not do anything with it."[1]

The same holds true for the way we treat other people. My adaptation of Peck's warning is others-centric: "Until you value people, you won't value their time. Until you value their time, you won't protect it."

I go out of my way to protect my database of givers' time. One example is in how I deal with introductions. These days most introductions take place digitally. Rather than a cold email connection, I prefer to show up filled up, even via my inbox.

When someone introduces me via email, I make sure I integrate these six steps:

1. **One and Done**: I reply all, but I Bcc my friend. I want my friend to know I followed up with his/her contact. This communicates respect to my friend, and it provides accountability to the new contact in case she says I didn't follow up with her. My very first line of the email is:

    _____ (Friend's Name) is Bcc to protect his/her time.

2. **Edify Your Friend**: I say something brief, specific, and complimentary about my friend. Few things honor someone as much as edifying him in front of the person he introduced you to. This gesture also says a ton about the caliber of person you are.

3. **Your Friend = My Friend**: Tell the person you just met that because she is important to your friend, that she is now important to you too. This new contact just entered your inner circle by association. Naturally, this new contact will feel valued because of their newly attained privileged position.

4. **Do (a little) Homework**: Next, I do a little research on the new contact. In my email response, I include a sincere compliment related to his book, website, or business. I might listen to a few minutes of his podcast, read a few pages of his book via the "Look Inside" feature, or

watch a few minutes of his video. This response immediately creates value for the new contact and my friend. It communicates genuine interest and authentic care. The new contact experiences how unique it feels for someone to show up filled up.

5. **Brand Match**: Most likely, this new contact is a brand match since she is connected to my friend. After my quick research in Step 4, if the new contact is a brand match, I make it a point to acknowledge that fact in my reply. Then I also Cc my strategic assistant and ask him to schedule us for a meeting. If you don't have an assistant, be sure to include a link to your booking calendar. This is another gesture that demonstrates competence to your friend and your new contact. It sets the tone for expectations regarding time and efficiency.

6. **Value-Based Signature**: I include an email signature that adds value to the new contact. Currently, my email signature includes a featured interview I did for *Entrepreneur Magazine* titled: How Your Story Can Generate 18 Streams of Income in Under 90 Days with Kary Oberbrunner. In addition to the four-minute read, the article also includes a thirty-seven-minute video with multiple case studies and cutting-edge tips and strategies. My signature also includes a two-minute overview of our services at Ethos Collective and how we help influencers turn their wisdom into wealth through writing, publishing, and marketing

their book the right way. This signature not only educates the new contact before they hop on a call with a team member or me, but it also positions my friend with incredible clout for connecting them with a qualified expert who is committed to showing up filled up.

These six steps might seem lengthy. Once you do it a few times, however, you will discover that the efficiency of the process reduces the entire exchange to less than five minutes. By implementing templates and formatting your signature, the only step that takes more than one minute is skimming their content.

In this short amount of time, I can create an incredible amount of value for my friend and for the new connection. It doesn't take much effort, but it does require sincerity and a love for helping others to show up filled up for everyone.

I have a similar (even shorter) process for making introductions via email:

1. **Stellar Subject Line**: Don't waste words.

   The subject line you choose is just as important as the first words of a book or the first seconds of a movie. This is why I make the introduction interesting and edifying. As an example, if I am introducing a new contact named Suzy to my friend Dave who produces audiobooks, I might use one of these three subject lines:

   Hey superstars—Time you both meet (goodness begins now)

Author Extraordinaire meet My Audiobook
Expert
Suzy and Dave = Souls on Fire

2. **Edify Your Friend**: I start the email with a brief, specific, and complimentary note about my friend. As I mentioned above, few things honor someone as much as edifying him in front of the person he introduced you to. This gesture also says a ton about the caliber of person you are. In the second line of the email, I say something about the new contact. Besides mentioning the person's superpower, I also state what he needs and why I am connecting him with my friend. This is not only helpful, but it also shows that you respect both of their time.

3. **In and Out**: After a super brief introduction of three lines, tell them that you are opting out of the email chain. Nothing beneficial transpires by you getting copied on multiple follow-up messages. In fact, including you removes the bliss of connecting people. Subconsciously, you'll be less likely to tap into your database of givers if the new connection includes too much friction. This is why I literally say at the end of the email:

I'll let you two take it from here and remove myself from the conversation. Enjoy the new connection. You're both amazing.

Bonus Tip: Don't ever send out a large group email and Cc everyone's email address. This gesture erodes credibility and trust in seconds.

Many influencers go out of their way to protect their email addresses. I've seen people lose relationships over email address inclusion on large emails. If you still don't get the rationale, think of it as on par with writing someone's personal cell phone number on a bathroom stall (not cool).

Know who you're looking for.

One of the joys of building a database of givers and connectors at your fingertips is that you'll discover a new sense of freedom. Let me explain: You can't help everyone. Neither can you work with everyone—nor should you. Besides, not everyone will be the right fit for you or your business.

Our goal is to be intentional about attracting and connecting with right-fit people. On topic, we must be just as intentional about letting go of the people who *aren't* the right fit.

Very often, a person's character—the truth about who they are—is revealed at the point of sale. It's incredibly important to remain attentive during the "close." If something feels off during these exchanges, listen to your instincts and press the pause button.

Not long ago, I connected with a potential client. After our meeting, I received three additional emails from him. Here's what he said in those follow-up emails:

- Hey, we're different from all your other clients.

- We have a niche market unlike anyone you've ever worked with.

- We don't want you to get paid based upon the work you do. We want to pay you based on your performance.

The idea of getting paid based on results doesn't scare me—quite the opposite. I'm deeply committed to producing results. His comments, however, were red flags, warning me about our working relationship before it even began.

If this is how it is before we even start, then I don't even want to work with this guy, I thought. If those three emails were any indication of the kind of working relationship we would have, things would be incredibly uncomfortable moving forward. Recognizing this, I hit the pause button and told the potential client that my company was not the best fit for his needs and desires.

In other words, I said, "No, thank you," to the relationship.

Showing up filled up requires drawing tough lines at times. It means giving yourself permission to say no to the types of clients and relationships that aren't right for you and your company. You don't need to be rude. Simply say, "I must admit that I'm not the best person to serve you. The good news is that I know someone who may be able to help you the right way."

When you become just as intentional about saying no to the wrong-fit people as you are to saying yes to the right-fit people, you will discover that you have greater strength and more bandwidth. This means you'll be able to help even more people.

Don't rescue or create codependency.

Trying to be all things to all people and attempting to be the answer to everyone's problem weakens your value. Showing up filled up means you know your boundaries and your worth. When you're the wrong match for someone, you do your new prospect a disservice by faking it.

When you recognize you can't rescue someone from their problem or help them with their goals, direct them toward someone who can. You might think this turns you into a high-traffic doormat, but that is so far from the truth. Think of your role as a door instead. You only open "your door" for the people you can serve well.

Hold the door open wide for the people who you believe in and for the people who believe in you. Be their hero. As you foster positive, mutually beneficial connections, you are sure to discover more than a few heroes in your database of givers.

CHAPTER 5

Broadcast Belief

You generate an unlimited supply
of value, goodwill, and belief.

At the age of eighteen, I was done with life. After suffering three unexpected disappointments—one after the other—I gave up. I screamed to the universe that I couldn't take one more loss. Then I went inside myself to deal with the heavy blows. Self-injury became my only escape.

Along came a stranger by the name of Carl Munenzmaier, the man I mentioned in the introduction. He sent me a letter with $500 and told me he believed in me. He said God needed me and couldn't afford to have me discouraged.

I borrowed Carl's belief in me because I had none of my own. His belief literally shaped the trajectory of my life. It's why, to this day, I sign all of my books, "I believe in you."

I think most people desperately need someone else to believe in them. The popular quote often attributed to Blaise Pascal speaks so powerfully of this need: "I bring you the gift of these four words: I believe in you."

Everyone could use an extra-large heaping of belief. This is why when someone comes along who sincerely believes in you, they immediately become an outlier. Self-belief is already rare, but belief granted to you by someone else is rarer still.

Carl was one of the first people I met—outside of my family—who showed up filled up. He knew the secret and used it. Because of his gift of belief, my life is different. More to the point, I'm still alive because he gave me the gift of his belief in me.

This mantra—show up filled up—isn't some gimmick or slogan. It's a way of life that saves lives.

The reason? Belief has an odor.

Unbelief has an odor, and people can smell it. Belief does too.

My editors are amazing. They told me I might want to change the word odor in this section. They said it could be misconstrued. I understand their rationale. Odor is often associated with an unpleasant smell. The dictionary, however, defines odor as "a *distinctive* smell."

This is the exact definition of unbelief AND belief. Both have a *distinct* smell. The truth is, I can smell unbelief on a person from a mile away. The same is true with belief. Put me in a room with someone who truly believes, and I can "sniff" them out in seconds.

You can too.

In the past few years, we experienced scary times with the global health crisis. Along with these events came the unending supply of fear, political divide, and economic scarcity. These topics dominated the headlines for months, and soon it was the only subject people talked about.

We saw firsthand that false news spreads faster (six times faster) than actual news. The general public became infected with misinformation, pessimism, and cynicism.[1] The virus of *fear* proved to be more deadly than any real physical virus, claiming the lives of countless people worldwide through depression, suicide, and anxiety.

This unbelief has an odor, and people can smell it right away. Who wants to do business with a pessimist? If your supplier, vendor, or coworker "smells" of fear, then their future looks quite dim. Innovation and collaboration are based upon the future. When you obsess about projecting a dark future, no one wants to do business with you. After all, if you're going under, why would people commit to your product or service? It's a bad investment, plain and simple.

Emitting a different type of smell isn't as easy as dousing yourself with perfume. Rather, it originates from a place deep within. Conviction and commitment must mix with integrity and character.

In 2020, we all experienced doubt and fear. None of us had ever been through a worldwide crisis of this magnitude before. But showing up filled up means dealing with your doubts offline. What good comes from going live with your fears in real-time on social media? Plenty of people did it, and they smelled like everyone else.

Thankfully, not everyone succumbed to the panic. Some chose to broadcast belief instead. Our company was one of these exceptions. Like everyone else on Planet Earth, we, too, had a choice of what to focus on. We could regurgitate the unending diet of doom and gloom and "smell" like everyone else. Or we could choose to tell a different story.

Our response was to turn my spring break at a private beach house into a free global online conference. We went live every day, twice a day, for an entire week. I interviewed celebrities, coaches, thought leaders, authors, musicians, and athletes. Each guest poured out their hearts with hope, faith, and love.

While the world was falling apart all around us, a gathering of people offered an antidote. We smelled differently, and people noticed. The Igniting Souls tribe broadcasted belief, and lives were changed.

In my favorite book, the author talks about being an outlier. He didn't use the words "show up filled up." Rather, he told us to be the salt and light of the world:

You are the salt of the earth. But if the salt loses its saltiness, how can it be made salty again? It is no longer good for anything except to be thrown out and trampled underfoot.

You are the light of the world. A town built on a hill cannot be hidden. Neither do people light a lamp and put it under a bowl. Instead, they put it on its stand, and it gives light to everyone in the house. In the same way, let your light shine before others, that they may see your good deeds and glorify your Father in heaven.[2]

Without salt and light, life becomes very bland and dark. For many people, bland and dark were the definition of their 2020, and they paid the price with mental and emotional illness. Their unbelief smelled of death and disease.

On the flip side, others took this global crisis and redeemed it by broadcasting belief. They showed up filled up, became outliers, and fought back with faith, belief in themselves and others, and powerful acts of love. In doing so, they inoculated themselves and those within their circle of influence from the effects of fear.

Responding to the real threats of life with belief and positive action requires that we evaluate our circumstances with clarity—something we can't do when our mind is clouded with fear. Some people will look at our belief and call it shortsighted optimism. But the truth is, it doesn't matter if the glass is half full or half empty. In the words of my friend and teammate Brenda Haire, we must see the glass as *refillable*.

We behave as realists who believe we can shape the future. When your belief is real, that's exactly what you'll do.

Don't keep score.

Those who know and practice the secret of showing up filled up don't keep score. Jill Young is this type of person.

Before I met Jill, I heard about her. I didn't know it at the time, but I learned much later that she heard about me before we met too. (Think back to the principle from the Introduction: Let your reputation precede you.)

A few years ago, my business was growing quickly—too quickly. I always loved being the visionary, but over time a leadership vacuum emerged. The person serving as our integrator at the time could no longer implement the ideas as quickly as we needed. As a result, I served in both roles: visionary and integrator. This worked for several years, but then I ended up resenting my life. At the time, I couldn't understand why, but today the reason is crystal clear.

The pattern went like this. I would get excited and create a new vision. Then I had to turn around and integrate the vision. When I finally integrated the vision, I was exhausted. The way I'm wired, I find new life by creating a new vision. But in taking on both roles, I knew that the moment I cast a vision, I would be the one responsible for integrating it. I dreaded the integration process, so I grew weary of the vision the moment I created it.

This cycle sucked the life out of me, and I could no longer show up filled up for my life, my family, or my team.

I knew something had to give. Around that time, my friend David handed me a book called *Rocket Fuel* by Gino Wickman and Mark C. Winters and encouraged me to read it. Once I did, my eyes were opened to the reality of my situation. I realized I wasn't going crazy and that I didn't hate my life. What I hated was the unnecessary burden I had created by trying to be the visionary *and* the integrator. It was simply too much. Besides, I was *created* to be a visionary, not an integrator.

According to *Rocket Fuel*, "Visionaries have groundbreaking ideas. Integrators make those ideas a reality. This explosive combination is the key to getting everything you want out of your business. It worked for Disney. It worked for McDonald's. It worked for Ford. It can work for you."[3]

I examined the back of the book and saw that it was associated with EOS®. Through my relationship with Dan Sullivan and Strategic Coach®, I had heard the term EOS® many times. I thought it was some kind of software program. A deeper exploration revealed the meaning of the letters: Entrepreneurial Operating System®. It is "a complete set of simple concepts and practical tools that has helped thousands of entrepreneurs get what they want from their businesses."[4]

I didn't know how EOS® worked or what it could do for me or my company, but the name Jill Young kept popping up in multiple conversations. After a little more digging, I learned she was a Certified EOS® Implementer, someone who would work with leaders to implement EOS® in their businesses. A colleague told me, "You'll never be able to get Jill. She's the best, and she's expensive. Besides, she's completely booked."

I always love a challenge, so I thought: *Game on.* I researched her company online and then sent her team an email. They responded that she was not available for two weeks.

A few hours later, she emailed me and said she had an opening the next day to chat. She told me that mutual friends had told her to connect with me and that my superpower was publishing and marketing. I blocked the appointment for the following day and then went to work, purchasing her audiobooks and studying her website.

I understood I only had twenty-four hours to learn everything about how I could help her. I created a slide deck and outlined a strategy to increase her influence, impact, and income with her current books and maybe even future books.

When we hopped on the chat, she asked me how she could help. I showed up filled up and turned the tables. I asked questions about her goals, dreams, and desires. I took note of her vision and how she saw her books interfacing with her business.

After about forty minutes, she said, "This is amazing. You keep serving me. I'm supposed to be the one helping you. Before we go any further, I want to know what I can do for you."

I took a deep breath and asked her for permission to continue. I asked her if she really wanted me to go deep and share everything. She replied with an enthusiastic, "YES!"

Recognizing her passion and sincerity, I then went on a ten-minute explanation about how I read *Rocket Fuel* and how I wanted to be a visionary again and implement EOS® in our business. She listened, commented, and probed. Then she said, "Now I have a question for you. Do I have your permission?"

I reciprocated with a resounding, "YES!"

She replied, "Are you ready to let go of control and allow your business to grow up?"

Her words seared my soul. I knew what she was asking, and it wasn't a trivial question. I looked into the future and saw the people who would leave the company. I realized how everything would shift, especially life as I knew it. I took a deep breath, completely understanding the weight of my reply.

"I am ready!" I said.

"Great," she said. "Where do we go from here?"

I told her about a crazy idea that I had. In the words of Dan Sullivan, I asked her if she wanted to create a Free Zone Frontier. She would become our EOS® Implementer, and I would become her publisher. Since we were both cash confident and committed to out-serve the other person, no money would be exchanged. We wouldn't keep score. We would, instead, keep adding value to each other's business and brand.

Our friendship and collaboration have evolved in so many amazing and mutually beneficial ways. Imagine two people and two businesses committed to show up filled up. We've referred new clients to each other. I've launched her books. She's spoken on my stage.

We both provide each other immense value, and our Free Zone is worth so much more than a dollar sign. It's an incredible experience when two people show up filled up for each other like this. I take care of her cover design, interior formatting, global distribution, and ISBNs. She keeps all the profits from her books. Then Jill takes care of all the business coaching and retreats that have brought Igniting Souls Publishing Agency to an entirely new level. We keep all of our profit.

This works beautifully because neither of us keeps score about what we do for the other. We keep giving the other person more value and receiving more value in return. It works because neither of us is trying to be a taker. We came into the relationship with the goal of helping each other, and it has transformed so many other readers, teams, and businesses in the process.

This is the power of partnering with other people committed to showing up filled up.

Stay top of mind.

You might have noticed in my initial connection with Jill, neither of us had to sell. My reputation had preceded me, just as her reputation preceded her. Our mutual connections had relayed stories of our successes.

The stories did the selling on our behalf.

So many people tell me they hate selling. The good news is that when you show up filled up, you don't need to focus on selling. You focus on storytelling instead. There's a big difference between the two.

By telling stories, we talk about our client's success rather than our own. Listeners can see themselves in our story. In fact, a good storyteller creates space for the listeners. They rationalize, *If it worked for that person, then it could work for me too.*

This is why I include so many case studies in my webinars. I share examples of children's authors, business authors, fiction authors, and fitness authors. The more stories I tell, the more programs I sell.

Even if people don't buy that day, a good story sticks with them and keeps you top of mind.

A while back, I found out that one of our client's books was featured in an Australian library. I took a screenshot of this information and sent it as a text message to the author. I quickly received a reply thanking me for the news.

That's it. Nothing more. Right?

Of course not.

The possibilities from that one quick text message are endless. My author could have been having lunch with a friend. She could have looked at her phone and said, "Oh, my gosh! My book just got picked up in Australia!"

If her friend wants to write a book (eighty-two percent of the population does), this text message could bring that desire front and center.

- She might reason that if her friend can write a book, she can too.

- She might inquire about me as a publisher.

- She may ask for the website address to our free author webinar (KaryOberbrunner.com/Book).

- She may join our publishing program.

- She might start writing a book on her journey of overcoming postpartum depression.

- She may publish that book six months from now.

A woman battling depression may read the book, find hope, and choose life rather than suicide. Her new little baby may go on to have a mother rather than grow up guilty her mother took her life because of her birth into the world.

If those possibilities sound oddly specific, it's because stories like this have happened—simply because I sent one text message and stayed top of mind!

Showing up filled up means adding value to everyone you meet.

Changing lives is simply a byproduct.

Every interaction is a deposit or a withdrawal.

After every interaction with another person, ask yourself:

Did I give, or did I take?

Those who show up filled up are self-aware enough to know the difference.

Similar to a bank account, when you have a positive effect on someone else, you make a deposit. When you have a negative effect on someone else, you make a withdrawal.

In a real sense, every interaction deposits value or withdraws value. Naturally, your goal is to raise your value. Although you can't control the other person's perception, you can control your actions. Givers keep making regular deposits when it's convenient and even when it's not.

Repel people who broadcast scarcity and complaints.

Be warned. Not everyone appreciates people who show up filled up.

If you choose to use this secret, you'll repel people who want to stay stuck in their ways. Complainers, haters, and blamers will feel threatened. Of course, they won't admit it. They'll direct their energy at tearing you down instead. They'll say, "*Who does this person think they are?*"

Don't waste your time or effort on sideways energy.

Whether you are a person of faith or not, Jesus Christ gives us a great example of someone who showed up filled up wherever he went, especially for his twelve disciples.

What was the result?

- Judas rejected him.

- Peter denied him.

- James and John fell asleep when he needed them most.

- All twelve ran for their lives when Jesus was arrested.

How did Jesus respond? With gossip, anger, frustration, or rage? Nope. He kept showing up filled up, and he eventually won many of them back.

Remember, you're responsible *to* people and not *for* people. There's a huge difference between the two. I've been misjudged and underestimated by plenty of people. Some left me for good, but others came back with an apology or a confession.

A woman recently said to me, "When I met you, I said, 'This guy can't be for real.' And then I left. But now I've come back because I just couldn't shake it. I now realize you're the real deal."

When criticism comes, remind yourself showing up filled up means detaching yourself from the outcome. If people broadcast scarcity and complaints, let them go. You won't need to disqualify them because they'll disqualify themselves by walking away. This gives you even more bandwidth to invest in the people who are hungry for what you have to offer.

CHAPTER 6

Less Is More

*You stand out because of what
you don't say and don't do.*

A dding value is both an art and a science. It's not about how loud you shout. Oftentimes, getting people's attention is a result of what you *don't* do and what you *don't* say. Those who show up filled up recognize that less is more.

Think back to my time in London when I approached the speakers. I didn't talk about myself, my credentials, or my list of clients. I focused on the speaker in front of me. *Less is more*—those three words encapsulated that experience.

Ludwig Mies van der Rohe coined the term "less is more," and he manifested it through his minimalist architecture. Decades later, this mindset has crept into our everyday lives, becoming so integrated into our conversations it almost seemed to come from nowhere. Now, it can be seen in entertainment, advertising, and corporate America.[1]

In this chapter, you'll discover several tips that will help you show up filled up. A word of warning: Don't let the simplicity fool you. Most people make these rookie mistakes and repel incredible opportunities. If you see yourself in these examples, don't feel guilty. I've made every single mistake, multiple times.

If I can learn to adapt, you can too.

Do your research.

Never ask an influencer something you can Google.

When you make a request, you withdraw "credibility chips." Some requests are worth the withdrawal. Asking an influencer how to turn on your webcam is not one of them.

By doing your research *before* you engage with someone, you're able to show up filled up.

Just the other day, I was on a call with a world-famous dentist. Because his profession was out of my wheelhouse, I invested a few minutes doing some research on him. When we chatted later that day, I mentioned some facts about him I'd just read online.

He stopped and asked me, "How did you know that? Wow! You must have done your research!"

My small gesture gave me an opportunity to show my potential client how much I cared about him. By his own admission, it left an impression. He said, "You know what? I hired someone to help me with some marketing, and they didn't take the time to learn anything about me." He could tell within the first few minutes I was excited to work with him because I had already done my research.

Showing up filled up means you don't walk into an interaction empty-handed. You show up prepared. And because you prepared for the moment, the moment is prepared for you.

It's similar to how a doctor walks into a treatment room with your file in hand, ready to talk about your medical history. She walks in and says, "I understand you've been experiencing some shoulder pain since you fell off that ladder two weeks ago. Tell me: How are you feeling today?"

Boom!

All it takes is a few seconds of prep time *before* she walks into the room to show you she cares. As a patient, you feel incredibly valued. It's a simple practice that costs very little, but it can add significantly to your credibility account.

Integrate associations.

Like you, I have many connections on social media. Whenever I get a new friend request, I go to the person's profile to see how many connections we have in common. Big Tech companies know the power of associations and social proof. If someone shares a common friend, then we're more likely to trust the other person.

No mutual friends. No mutual trust.

In my publishing business, with a few clicks, I can see which of my past clients are connected to other big players in the industry. When I meet this new connection, I can engage him or her in a conversation about the friend I published.

I don't need to spend time proving myself or selling our services. I let associations do that for me.

Less is more.

Make others the heroes, not how you helped them.

Justin Donald is one of our authors who made No. 1 on the *Wall Street Journal* bestseller list, even beating out Barak Obama's book. I tell his story often, especially on discovery calls with prospective clients. He became a hero to people in the lifestyle investment industry, and I love to shine the spotlight on his success.

When you show up filled up, you don't need to talk about yourself. You make room for others to step onto the stage where you can share their story, just as I do with Justin.

Knowing the secret of showing up filled up and using the secret means you have enough self-confidence to step aside and make room for others to shine. The people around you will take notice and recognize that there's something different about you.

Dr. Pat Luse is another hero I like to showcase. His book, *The 7 Systems Plan*, has transformed peoples' health all around the world. Though my team helped Dr. Pat on his success journey, we never position ourselves as the heroes but rather the guides. Donald Miller, the author of *StoryBrand*, says, "Always be the guide, never the hero."[2]

Affirm their value and contributions.

People have an innate desire to feel helpful.

When I'm on a sales call, if the other person says something that's incredibly smart, I make a big deal about it. I stop the meeting and write down what they said. I've always been a lifelong learner, and I get excited when I learn something new.

When you show up filled up, you open the door for someone else to impact your life. You create space for someone to teach you. Only empty people pretend they have everything figured out.

Many times, people ask me difficult questions, some of which I don't know the answer. I have several choices in this type of situation.

1. I could lie and fabricate a response.

2. I could say, "I don't know," and end the conversation.

3. I could promise to find the answer for them.

This third response immediately creates trust. We only lose credibility when we pretend and hide. But when we admit we don't know, the other person senses our sincerity. They realize we care enough to be open and honest.

Protect confidentiality.

Never gossip about a past client in front of a current client.

When you do, then you tell everyone within earshot you're ready, willing, and able to gossip about them someday too. The way you treat your past client is a reflection of how you're going to treat your future client. If a current client hears you gossiping about others, he stops and thinks, *If she talks this way about others, what will she say about me?*

If a situation arises where you need to bring up negative information about a past client as a case study or illustration, always protect their confidentiality. Don't use the person's name. Go out of your way to protect the details. When your potential client sees how you protect someone's confidentiality, he or she immediately gains a deeper level of respect for you. The potential client will more than likely go out of their way to protect your confidentiality if and when the opportunity ever presents itself.

You never gain anything from gossiping about someone else. It only presents you in a negative light. Even on the topic of gossip, remember—less is more.

CHAPTER 7

Becoming Valuable Makes You Visible

*You become irreplaceable and
therefore priceless.*

When you look around, you'll notice a short supply of people who genuinely show up filled up. These *transformational* types are *outliers.* Maybe you're one of them.

Other people are willing to help, but they expect something in return. These *transactional* types are *average.*

Still, others entirely ignore the call to be helpful.

Because of this shortage, the upside is incredible. If you show up filled up, you have an opportunity to stand out. By being valuable, you'll become visible. Make it a lifestyle, and the world will sit up and take notice.

When this happens, you become *irreplaceable*.

In this chapter, you'll learn how to become irreplaceable—a transformational outlier.

Defer your ask.

When people first learn this secret, naturally, they get excited—and they should. Initially, they think about the short game and how they're only a few steps away from everything they've ever wanted.

They think, *I'm going to help someone, and then— boom—I'll get whatever I want before the day is done.* With this approach, relationships dissolve before they even begin.

When you serve someone, it's natural for them to offer to return the favor. Most of us grew up with this mindset of reciprocation. You help me, then I help you. The essence of a transactional relationship is stating your request immediately so the other person can "get even" by returning the favor.

My suggestion is to take a different approach. Defer the ask and respond instead by showing up filled up even more. When you don't immediately ask for something in return, you get inside the other person's head. People don't know what to do. They certainly don't want the relationship to end. In fact, they feel indebted to you. This is when serious transformation takes place.

People desperately want to get even, especially if they're the type used to giving rather than receiving. They might say, "Listen, you've helped me so much. What can I do for you in return?"

You might be tempted to name your favor, but I encourage you to mix up your approach. Instead of asking, say something like this: "I'm good. It's my honor to help. I don't need anything." Then don't let the relationship go stagnant. Keep pouring on the value.

By deferring your request, you give the relationship time and space to develop and strengthen.

Remain unattached to the outcome.

There comes a time when you need to convert your courage into "the ask." As your relationship continues to grow, you'll eventually want to take it to a deeper level. Perhaps this means presenting a request, a favor, or a collaboration.

Many people fear this step, and that's actually a great sign. It signifies the relationship means something to you. Healthy fear results from the thought of losing the relationship—or at least experiencing a change in the relationship. Making an ask involves real risk. If you don't feel any fear, then you should question whether you've invested enough in the other person at this point in time.

Think about it. These past six chapters, you've grown in your self-awareness. Before you learned the secret of showing up filled up, you were ignorant. You didn't fear asking anyone for anything because it didn't matter if he or she said no. You had nothing to lose because you hadn't invested anything yet.

But everything changes when you invest in other people. Now you care about them, their feelings, and their future. It's okay to feel the fear, but make your request known anyway. By showing up filled up, playing the long game, and deferring the ask in the short term, you've demonstrated your commitment. You're not going anywhere, and neither is the other person.

Here's a quick tip: When you feel the fear, tell your mind that your body is simply excited. Redefine the anxiety as adrenaline. By reinterpreting your apprehension, you'll step into the moment and show up filled up even more. This psychological stretch is a preloading phase to get you into *flow*—the optimal state of human performance. (For more on this topic, refer to my book: *Unhackable*.)

Although your "ask" carries weight, it's important to remain unattached to the outcome. Showing up filled up means you don't force your agenda. Make your presence known, but don't push the other person away. Speak with clarity and conviction, but if the timing isn't right, be prepared to redirect your energy. It might sound odd, but I picture myself as a strong stream of water. Whenever an obstacle appears in my path, I simply find my way around it.

Remember, showing up filled up doesn't mean one and done. The essence of transformational relationships is change, and sometimes the other party isn't ready for change. No matter, you keep pouring on the value. The influencer isn't about to lose you and your relationship. You're priceless and irreplaceable. Now more than ever, renew your loyalty. It will go a long way, especially in light of the "temporary" rejection you may feel.

This was my recent experience with an incredible influencer. I earned a sizable amount of trust and goodwill serving a particular company for several years. I made it a point to show up filled up with every interaction. They hired me for multiple publishing projects and referred their clients to me.

The day came for me to present a proposal for a new product line that would earn their company tens of millions of dollars. I prepared mentally for this moment for months and invested over twenty hours in designing a bulletproof presentation.

Finally, the day arrived for me to share my plan with her. Halfway through the presentation, I could tell something was wrong. I felt a barrier between us. Was it something I said? Or something I did?

I paused—knowing there was no advantage to keep pushing.

She broke the silence. "You know, this sounds very interesting, but . . ."

Then, she went on to tell me about a recent relationship where her trust was broken. The pain in her voice was fresh and palpable. Although she didn't share details, she mentioned how it was significant—enough to warrant a legal battle.

I stepped into a storm I didn't create and one I couldn't help repair. This was sideways energy, and showing up filled up in this moment meant shutting up. My presentation was no longer salvageable.

Earning more influence would only be achieved by abandoning my plan.

"You know what?" I said. "I completely understand. It's not the right time or the right idea for you. I'm not going anywhere. I will have plenty of ideas in the future. But you won't hear from me on this particular idea again."

Then I smiled and shut up.

She looked a little taken aback at my abrupt stop. Then she said, "Wow, you're good. I've never seen anyone pivot like that before."

I reaffirmed my respect for them and their company. I told them if it's not good for them, then it's not good for me. We ended the conversation soon after, with a few sincere pleasantries.

For a few minutes after the video conference had ended, I sat in my chair, stunned. Part of me felt proud I had just weathered this storm without falling apart on camera. I knew the timing of my plan couldn't be worse for them, but not as a result of anything I did.

"Nooooo!!!" I yelled, sitting in my office. "This sucks! This ab-so-lute-ly SUCKS!"

Since my entire team is remote, nobody heard the guttural yawp I shot into the air. Nonetheless, expelling my primal angst had a cathartic effect.

My heart was set on this idea. I saw how everything about my plan ticked off every box this company's leaders needed to achieve their big vision. Yet I knew no amount of coaxing or cajoling would bring them around.

Clinging to my idea would only drive them further away. So I invited myself—and only myself—to a five-minute pity party. Then I brushed myself off. I've never brought up the idea since. I stayed unattached to the outcome.

Three months later, another opportunity emerged for me to serve this company in even greater ways. Because I had remained fluid, I remained relevant to them. Even after my self-perceived loss—the rejection of my proposal—I created a big win by focusing on what's best for them, not what's exciting for me.

Be clear, concise, and direct.

Never waste your words.

I meet too many people who make this mistake. Do your thinking *before* your speaking and *before* your emailing. Influencers don't have time to hear you try to communicate yourself into clarity. When you do, you show up empty.

If you need to talk something out first, do this with a trusted friend or colleague. Make a positive impression by making your conversations what my friend Chet Scott calls CCD: Clear, Concise, Direct.

I've had to integrate my own advice, even with this book.

Show Up Filled Up is the shortest book I've ever written. This is intentional. In our attention economy, clear, concise, and direct is more powerful, valuable, and practical, especially in a world where human knowledge is doubling every twelve hours. I want you, my reader, to understand and apply this secret. Therefore, it's on me to deliver it in the simplest form.

Think of the alternative: ULI—Unclear, Lengthy, Indirect. This approach is guaranteed to repel influencers. It's lazy, selfish, and impractical.

We must do the deep work in the dark so we can stand confidently in the light. Before you try to help someone, you must discover the answers on your own.

Let your yes be yes and your no be no.

Back in 2001, the NBA asked U2 to play at the NBA Finals halftime show. By chance, the band was giving a concert at another location down the road in Boston, the same city as the finals. The basketball league wanted one of the biggest bands of all time to go live on national TV for a few minutes right before a commercial break.

There was just one small catch.

Since basketball games never go according to schedule due to timeouts, fouls, and free throw shots, the NBA required that U2 go on temporary standby as halftime neared. Tens of thousands of concert fans would need to wait patiently. The TV producers would give the signal when to go live, and U2 would break into a song from their concert hall a few miles away from the basketball court.

U2 would receive a large amount of money for their halftime entertainment. The band would get worldwide exposure, and the concert fans would be inconvenienced for a few minutes while U2 waited for the signal.

But that signal never came.

Bono refused the offer. He didn't need to consult the rest of the band members. Bono wouldn't alter his concert, even for a large sum of money. His loyalty to his fans was more important than a paycheck. He gave them a firm "no." If the NBA wanted to broadcast the show, they would need to cut in and join the concert wherever the band might be in their setlist.[1]

The NBA compromised and agreed to the terms.

When the TV station showed a live feed of the concert, viewers everywhere saw an incredible image of Bono on his knees praying. He said, "What can I give back to God for the blessings he poured out on me? I lift high the cup of salvation as a toast to our Father, to follow through on the promise I made to you."[2] Then the band played "Where the Streets Have No Name." This spontaneous moment couldn't have been any better. It was the climax of the concert, and the world watched in awe.

Bono had the courage to let his yes be yes and his no be no. This decision created an incredibly powerful moment. They got paid, the song was heard around the world, and it was a big win for everyone involved, especially their fans who got to witness that amazing moment. Bono could have lost the deal by saying no, but he valued his integrity and his loyalty to his fans more than money. His example of showing up filled up is one of the purest I've ever seen.

Overdeliver and own any shortcomings.

In your journey of leveraging this secret, you're going to make mistakes. None of us is perfect. I've made mistakes with my publishing clients, but I never made excuses or passed blame onto the team. I'm the CEO, and I take 100 percent responsibility for how everything goes down.

I welcome the opportunity to hear how we came up short. I strive to do everything in my power to correct any mistakes made along the way.

A few months ago, a situation of unmet expectations came to my attention. The client offered to share the risk with me fifty-fifty, but I refused. I knew I needed to own up to my responsibility, so I told that client we would pay for 100 percent of it. Even though I wasn't directly at fault, my reputation was on the line. Showing up filled up meant going out of my way to make it right.

CHAPTER 8

Convert Your Credibility into Currency

*You know the proper time
to strengthen the collaboration.*

Your wealth isn't measured by how much money you've made but rather by how much credibility you've earned. By showing up filled up, you'll earn more and more relational currency with each exchange. In this final chapter, you'll learn how to integrate this secret into a lifestyle where everyone you meet and everything you touch increases in value.

Create a game where everybody wins.

Many times in relationships, we think there should always be a winner and a loser. I disagree. I go out of my way to create a game where everybody wins.

In my world, this means making sure the author wins, the publisher wins, and the marketing team wins. I work to create deals that ensure everyone involved gets what they want. I make it a point to start with the end in mind regarding marketing, partnerships, businesses, and relationships.

In contrast, showing up empty keeps your focus on being the winner. But in that scenario, no one wins in the long run. Sure, you might win initially, but you also ruin your chances for long-term, mutually beneficial relationships.

Before you collaborate, start with this question: *What is my ultimate goal?* Then, break that down into smaller goals, identifying clear wins for all parties involved.

Define what success looks like.

I'm predictable—especially when it comes to meetings.

I ask the other people present, "What is the ideal outcome you want to achieve sixty minutes from now?" Then, I shut up and listen.

This approach makes sense for several reasons. First and foremost, it provides a deadline. If the end time isn't agreed upon, then there's no urgency. The mutually agreed-upon deadline creates movement and expectations.

Their response to the question matters too. Once you know how the other person defines success, you share a common scoreboard. Before these boundaries are set, you have no idea if you're making progress. Defining success with others invites them to operate from the same playbook. In a real sense, it's a commitment to get on the same page.

Share your platform with them.

Every person I've met wants to be recognized for what they're good at doing. One of the ways you can honor someone is by sharing your platform—no matter if it's big or small. By doing this, you offer value first.

Many times, I've brought other people onto my podcasts, live videos, and physical stages. Even when I had a small platform, I showed up filled up and honored my audience and the influencer. Don't wait until you have a big platform to become generous. Being generous now makes your platform bigger, *faster*.

Knowing the secret and using the secret is all about the other person, not you. Therefore, stand confidently on your platform, regardless of the size.

Repay them with your superpower.

You have a superpower, and hopefully, you know what it is.

If you're unsure, check out my Igniting Souls Trilogy: *Your Secret Name, The Deeper Path*, and *Day Job to Dream Job*. These books will help you get clarity around your Identity—who you are, Purpose—why you are here, and Direction—where you are going.

Once you know your superpower, use it generously to repay people for their contribution to your life.

When I invite people to speak at my conference, I oftentimes will offer them my superpower rather than an honorarium for their speaking fee. Most people prefer this rather than a check.

So what is my superpower? If you're hoping for X-ray vision, the ability to leap over a tall building, or flying into outer space, then you're going to be sorely disappointed.

My superpower, rather, is helping Authors, Coaches, Entrepreneurs, and Speakers (ACES) write, publish, and market their books the right way and turn them into eighteen streams of income.

Sometimes when speakers finish and the audience gives them a standing ovation, I hop on stage and announce their book deal with our company. The audience loves it because they feel as though they witnessed something amazing—something maybe nobody else in the world knows yet. The speaker feels honored, knowing there is a huge room of people already excited about their future book. It's a win-win-win.

Your superpower might not be publishing, but you do have one, and many people in the world need it. The more you master that superpower, the more value you can create for others. Show up filled up with that superpower, and suddenly you're irreplaceable.

Do what you wish they would do for you.

One of my mentors published a book this past year. Instead of asking my conference attendees to buy it when it came out, I bought them each a copy—all five hundred of them.

This was my mentor's first book, and I wanted to make him feel special. I said to him, "Listen, I want to purchase a copy of your book for everyone attending my conference. I will mail them out in special care packages, and your book will go out all over the world."

After I did this, I asked the attendees to take pictures holding his book and post them all over social media. The posts included words of affirmation and hashtags, and his book became a bestseller on several big lists.

Did this make a difference?

Absolutely!

Everyone's love made him feel like a million bucks. I didn't do this to make myself look like a hero. I did this because I wished someone had done this when I first started out as an author. Nobody did, so I struggled those first few years trying to build a successful career as an author.

Showing up filled up means doing for others what you wish they would do for you.

• • •

Before we end, one more word of warning.

Don't just learn the secret. Leverage it too.

We need a world where you help other people get what they want. Because when you do, you're able to get what you want.

Time to show up filled up.

I'm right here with you.

CONCLUSION

Show Up Filled Up as a Lifestyle

You show up filled up in every relationship and build a network where you're the buyer, not the seller.

Over the years, I've built this mindset into a mission. It's become my way of life.

When you show up filled up—in the words of Dan Sullivan—you become the buyer, not the seller.[1] The brutal truth is that no one wants to be around someone who's always selling.

You might wonder, *How can I make money if I never sell?* The answer is quite simple. Always serve.

People who don't get it stick out incredibly fast.

Once you learn the secret of showing up filled up, something powerful happens. Everyone else who acts otherwise sticks out.

I experienced this in Wisconsin last summer when visiting my parents. I set out for an early morning bike ride. Everything was perfect—until it wasn't. While riding up a hill, my back tire popped.

The spare tube didn't inflate properly. Here I was about twenty miles out, with no way to get back. Sure, I could have called my parents to pick me up, but I didn't want to inconvenience them.

I saw a Walmart® store across the street, so I walked inside. Upon entering, I asked the greeter to watch my bike for me since I had no lock. I journeyed throughout the store in my bike shorts, cycling shoes, and helmet. I wasn't sure what I was looking for—a tire repair kit or something I could rig to ride home.

A middle-aged man stopped me and offered a helping hand. He said, "I bet you have a flat. I live right down the road. Let me go grab some tubes, and I'll meet you back here to help you install them."

Talk about showing up filled up! This guy returned a few minutes later and started fixing my tire. Just then, a woman's screaming interrupted us. About thirty feet away, an irate woman cussed out the kind greeter who watched my bike a few minutes before.

Evidently, the store had run out of Diet Mountain Dew®, and this angry woman decided to unload her rage. I looked at her and then back at the guy helping me.

These two people couldn't be more different.

One gave value. The other took it away.

One became a hero. The other became a villain.

One showed up filled up. The other showed up empty.

Each of us has this choice every day. How will you choose to show up?

Technology keeps us honest.

Showing up empty is a liability, especially these days. We all have a video camera on our phones, and most people are more than willing to broadcast your behavior. Anyone could have easily taken a video of that woman at Walmart and shown the world what happens when you take your anger out on innocent people. These are the videos that go viral.

Her reputation could have been ruined over a twelve-pack of carbonated beverage. (I doubt it was worth it.)

Showing up filled up is more than a strategy. It's also a relational insurance policy.

Build a culture of showing up filled up.

My team recently attended an incredible training with Strategic Coach®. At the end of the session, the brilliant facilitator, Kristi Chambers, told me privately, "Your people are amazing! They come with batteries included." When I asked her to tell me more, she went on to explain. By her reply, I could tell she had caught the culture we commit to create wherever we go: showing up filled up.

Kristi didn't need to motivate or inspire my team because we've already internalized this show-up-filled-up lifestyle. It's who we are, not something we do.

Culture is contagious.

We call our community Igniting Souls. Many talented people leave other jobs to come work with our team. Some even give up higher-paying jobs because our culture is so contagious. They'd rather make less money and be around people they love who lift them up. We have to turn away great candidates because we have an overabundance of people passionate about doing work and life with us.

Showing up filled up is so important to me—to all of us—that we have made it one of our four core values. I'll list all four in order, just in case you are curious. Notice our four values spell GPS, and that's exactly what they are—a guide for where we are as a company.

1. Growth-Minded Grit

    • No Blame, Excuses, or Denial

    • Hunger to Win | We Keep Score

    • Lifelong Learner

    • Mentally Tough

2. Positive Optimism

    • The Glass Is Refillable

    • Ooze Abundance and Gratitude

    • The Obstacle Is the Way

    • We Shall Overcome

3. Show Up Filled Up

   - Own the Role / Self-Manager

   - Clarity, Competence, Confidence

   - Anticipate Needs

   - Problem Solver

4. Servant Leadership

   - Eager to Help

   - Serving Is Selling

   - No Drama or Sideways Energy, Just Truth-Telling

   - Connect with Creator, Core, and Community

The culture you create with your clients, for your team, for your family, and anyone else within your circle of influence matters. It's contagious. The good news is you get to decide what kind of culture to spread.

You are your marketing.

Many vendors and hotels vie for our annual conference business. Once they experience the Igniting Souls Conference attendees, they want us to return. We invest hundreds of thousands of dollars for rooms, food, and technology. Although we're technically the clients, our group takes on the role of the service provider.

At the end of our events, we bring the waitstaff, the sound technicians, the photographers, the production team, and the general manager on stage and give them a standing ovation. Although we write the checks, we celebrate the people who gave us value all week.

Remember, it's the little differences that make all the difference.

The choice is up to you, my friend. As my favorite book says, "Don't just be a hearer of the word. Be a doer too."[2]

You've *learned* the secret. Now it's time to *leverage* the secret. I look forward to hearing how you get what you want out of people and life by showing up filled up.

Share the Secret

I wish I would have learned this secret earlier in life. If I had, I could have helped many more people and ignited many more souls.

I have one simple request as we end our journey together. If this secret makes sense to you, please share it with the people you know.

Now more than ever, we need a world that shows up filled up.

I believe in you.

—Kary

Bibliography

Introduction
Cialdini, Robert B. *Influence: The Psychology of Persuasion*. New York: Harper Business, 2006.

Chapter 1
Mangold, James. *Walk the Line*. Fox 2000 Pictures, 2005.
Doyle, Sir Arthur Conan. "A Scandal in Bohemia." In *The Adventures of Sherlock Holmes*. London, England: George Newnes Ltd., 1892.

Chapter 2
Oberbrunner, Kary. Unhackable: *The Elixir for Creating Flawless Ideas, Leveraging Superhuman*

Focus, and Achieving Optimal Human Performance. Ethos Collective, 2020.

Wachowski, Lana and Lilly. *The Matrix*. Warner Brothers Entertainment Company, 1999.

Chapter 3

"The Toyota Method: A Shortcut for Identifying and Solving Your Problems." Accessed February 25, 2021. https://constantrenewal.com/toyota-method/.

Scott, Chet. Becoming Built to Lead: *Becoming Built to Lead: 365 Daily Disciplines to Master the Art of Living*. Ethos Collective, 2020.

Maxwell, John C. *The 21 Irrefutable Laws of Leadership: Follow Them and People Will Follow You.* Nashville: Thomas Nelson, 1998.

Scott, Chet. *Becoming Built to Lead: 365 Daily Disciplines to Master the Art of Living.*

Chapter 4

Peck, M. Scott. *The Road Less Traveled: A New Psychology of Love, Traditional Values and Spiritual Growth.* New York: Simon & Schuster, 1978.

Chapter 5

Dizikes, Peter. "Study: On Twitter, false news travels faster than true stories." Accessed May 10, 2021. https://news.mit.edu/2018/study-twitter-false-news-travels-faster-true-stories-0308.

Matthew 5:13–16, *Holy Bible,* NIV.

Wickman, Gino, and Mark C. Winters. *Rocket Fuel: The One Essential Combination That Will Get You More of What You Want from Your Business.* Dallas: BenBella Books, 2015.

"What is EOS®?" EOS Worldwide. Accessed May 7, 2021. https://www.eosworldwide.com/what-is-eos.

Chapter 6

Field Millburn, Joshua and Ryan Nicodemus. *Essential: Essays by The Minimalists.* Missoula, MT: Asymmetrical Press, 2015.

Miller, Don. *Building a StoryBrand: Clarify Your Message so Customers Will Listen.* New York: Harper Collins Leadership, 2017.

Chapter 7

Miller, Dan. "Would You Compromise for More Attention?" Accessed March 6, 2021. https://www.48days.com/would-you-compromise-for-more-attention/.

Beard, Steve. "Gratitude and the Rock of Ages." Accessed March 6, 2021. https://goodnewsmag.org/2019/11/gratitude-and-the-rock-of-ages/.

Conclusion

James 1:22, *Holy Bible*, paraphrased.

Sullivan, Dan. *Always Be The Buyer: Attracting other People's Highest Commitment to Your Biggest and Best Standards.* Author Academy Elite, 2019.

About the Author

KARY OBERBRUNNER is a *Wall Street Journal* and *USA Today* bestselling author and CEO of Igniting Souls Publishing Agency. Through his writing, speaking, and coaching, Kary helps individuals and organizations to clarify who they are, why they're here, and where they're going so they can become souls on fire.

Kary struggled to find his own distinct voice and passion. As a young man, he suffered from severe stuttering, depression, and self-injury. Today, a transformed man, Kary equips people to experience Unhackability in work and life and share their messages with the world. In the past twenty years, he's ignited over one million people with his content. He lives in Ohio with his wife, Kelly, and their three children.

Connect at KaryOberbrunner.com

Our mission is to help Authors, Coaches, Entrepreneurs, and Speakers (ACES) write, publish, and market their books the right way, and turn them into 18 streams of income.

You have a message to share and an audience to serve. Let us do everything else.

Chat with our team today.

IgnitingSoulsPublishingAgency.com

KO KARY OBERBRUNNER

Igniting Souls

The greatest rebellion is the one against your self-limiting beliefs.

KaryOberbrunner.com

Books | Podcast | Vlog

igniting**souls**

We believe:

Clarity attracts. Confusion repels.

There are two types of people in the world:
those that let the world happen to them and those
that happen to the world. Although a subtle difference,
this makes all the difference.

The glory of God is a person fully alive.
We were created to show up filled up.

The most powerful weapon on earth is the human soul on fire.
The most damaging thing in the life of a child is the
unlived life of a parent.

Souls on Fire know WHO they are (identity),
WHY they're here (purpose), and WHERE they're going (direction).

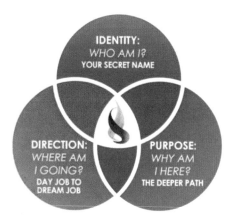

We help you write, publish, and market your book, then turn it into 18 streams of influence, impact, and income.

ethos
collective

EthosCollective.vip

Turn your wisdom into wealth.
Connect with us today.

Made in the USA
Columbia, SC
23 June 2021